dear,

Sydney Elise Johnson

dear,

A compilation of poems written by Sydney Elise Johnson
To you the fighter.
From me the conqueror.
For us the perfectly imperfect.

"One day, I'll paint the perfect sunset".

-Atticus

dear,

How I feel.

Gone

Don't be shocked
there is no light in
my eyes
in my
home
call the
electrician

~to those who killed my spirit

Palace

I'm only allowed to
feel what you want
me to feel./ pain

I'm only allowed to
be what you want
me to be./ empty

Welcome home

I have left a letter on the
kitchen table
signed
sincerely
because
you will not find me here

By the grace...

Silence is what I will
provide
because
nothing
is what you now
deserve

3:31 A.M.

//

You shoved paper into my palm
truculently placed
a pen in front of my face
I tried writing down my existence
there was no ink

Threatening

I should not have to put my body

in between yours and theirs

I should not have to act like a shield

just in case your bomb detonates

but I'd rather it hit me

than

them

No clarification

You do not
have to or
need to
explain why
you are
hurt
to the person
who keeps
hurting
you

Something to notice

You look at me with zero expectations but yet

expect me to arrive in a particular manner;

head held high, shoulders back, standing tall

as if I have agreed to rise to the occasion
//
you expect me to accept the fact that you deceived

me into living in an exhibit

mistaken as the world

Self-esteem

I'm

    afraid

I

    won't

          bloom

//

    like

you

    want

~to those who question their existence

Good will

I never expected loneliness to be my

most loyal companion

it's the one thing I can rely on to

always

be

here

Whiskey words

Your heaviness stabs its way through me
I woke up this morning and was
greeted with my tear stained pillow.
White sheets, white pillow, white comforter
no more.
I heaved my feet, burdened with your
whiskey fueled words and wounded slander
and trekked my body to my mirror.
The reflective glass seemed appetizing.

{The feeling of my jagged feet stomping against
the cold tiled floor in a place so familiar made me
feel alive even though you made me a corpse}

I looked.
Immediately cast judgement and deemed her as
a sufferer.
What I saw was not me; for I do not know who that
was.
Bloodshot eyes, sunken face, bruised heart.
I do not know who that was.
Guilt and pity made its face welcome.
I do not know who that was

but I wanted to reach out and touch her scars
with the softness she needed.
I do not know who that was,
but you did her wrong.

Peace

I'm the happiest when I hear your snoring
creeping through the floorboards
that
means I won't have to fight you
tonight

Continue

My wish for you
is that you continue
continue to be you
astonish a mean
cruel world with
your
kindness

Abandon

I get lost
in the
memories
that I
don't want
to
remember

I Still Love You

But

you

are

not

my

home

sweet

home

Half-empty

I rely on others
like a glass relies
on water to fill
it with life

how much
how little
how cold
how hot
it doesn't matter

the glass just wants to be
filled
with life
and
I
just want someone to fill me
with life

Acid shower

Last night, I left the door open
windows ajar and the storm came
rushing, rumbling in
the wind destroyed the vase and flowers
on the coffee table
rain soaked the wall into sludge
a tree fell and the lights
my lights went out

I

There is freedom waiting for you
until then
may the flowers remind you
why the thunderstorms are
necessary

Aftermath

I know you
the bundled
tangled
twisted
coiled
knotted
ball
of yarn
and people
are afraid
nervous
apprehensive
to unravel
your
knots

Know

That you are the most
difficult thing I have
ever seen

Fitting

Thinking about tomorrow
when today isn't over while
I'm still trying to understand
yesterday
makes me cry

regardless,
I always sit up in bed
today/tomorrow/yesterday
at midnight
crying

This morning

She can't get out of bed
because
your words left
bruises on her bones

Sadly

Living in a world
with you is
like
coming home to
a house that was
robbed
//
And hearing you
say to the police
*I didn't do anything
I made it better*

This is sincere

The morning after
you looted parts of
me
I woke up
and
I
wish I
didn't
//
this is
why I can't have
beautiful things

I guarantee

All the pain
heartache
and
heartbreak
is preparing you
for the kind of
love
that heals

Short story

I am not a recreational spot;
a place for your leisure, relaxation and amusement.
I am not a playground filled with your shattered memories
leaping from bar to bar, sliding down the slippery plastic
while you wait for my mind, my mind to become your
crestfallen childhood story.
I am the manifestation of my mother's wildest dreams.
I am not the gift you want but
I am the nourishment you need.
Do not come to my home in search for souvenirs.
My body is not for tourists.
I am not a doormat meant for your rough feet and filthy
shoes.
It isn't on display for your pleasure or perusal.
I am not on display
I am not for display.
//
I am not the debris and litter you see on the side of
the road on the way to your final destination.
I am the twinkling stars, the overpass, the street lights
that guide you to your getaway.
Without me there would be no destination and
Without me, you would never get there.

Dawn

Every morning she wakes
up to a storm
but she holds her breath
and endures the
hurricane

Questions part I

Are you okay
do you need
anything
water or
a bath
are you still
breathing
why can't you
remember
what time is
it and
have you eaten
did you stay
up all night
why aren't you
sleeping
what's wrong

Inside

A breathtaking anatomy of broken

Midnight thoughts

The thought of someone loving me
makes me afraid

I don't think of the happy memories
we could build along with the
house and white picket fence

I think of the pain
I think of the lies first presented as
truths
I think of the potential of the
nonexistent cheating and abuse

November 12.

Put a girl under the moon
and the stars and be
gentle with her heart
watch
her eyes will
finally
twinkle too

Absent gem

Do not fall in love with her
because of the dads
fathers and
father figures
she will break your heart
way before you get the
chance to know her name

Every time

Your presence
shoots shivers
down my
spine

Daily mistakes

I loved you.
I loved you hard
I loved you before I knew what
your mouth was capable of
you shackled my legs and burned
my feet
I cannot move
you killed me
and I still desired to love you
maybe
I shouldn't have

Weather, Whether

The sun made no promise to
you
me
her
him
them
to shine-
But it will whether we want it
to or not

Lost Boy

I chose to walk away
but I
left the door open
just
in case one night
I
decide to come
back
home

Everybody's something

In the darkness
//
but
when I touched
the light switch
your colors were
not what I
expected

At first

I thought my
forgiveness
would
change you
but it gave
you permission
to do
more damage

Stop

Looking for help
in someone who
watches you drown
from the shore

Honey

Queens make
rainbows out
of storms

Years ago

I let you into
my home and
forgot to
tell you to
wipe your
dirty feet

24/7

Things are wild and I don't know how
to tame
them
I grab a shovel to try to bury them
I paste on a smile to try to cover them
I soak in the bath to try to drown them

I close my eyes so my mind can't remember them

End chapter, same book

Watch
she smiled gently
but something was
different
her mouth smiled
but her eyes
did
not

5 months gone

5 months gone
I should not be
afraid to come
home

home: a house or shelter that is the usual residence
of a family; deep, to the heart

shelter: a place giving temporary protection from bad
weather or danger

temporary: lasting for only a limited period of time; not
permanent

Skewed analysis

Every time you say you love me I think of all of the awful things
you have said
and done
and if that's love then I want nothing to do with it

Bolted remembrance

Bodies in an old photograph
in a favorite coffee shop, long
gone
--a life I don't remember being a
part
of
//
But everyday, you remind me
that I was there
taking your order, carrying your
drinks, wiping down your table
paying for the mistakes you
made and choose to celebrate

Her
Get a shovel
and a bucket
or
a broom
and a dustpan
and pick
up your
pieces darling
because
no one else
will

Visitor

I have left my home, though I shouldn't
with hopes of finding a more tragic place
I leave behind footsteps in the mud, drenched
with my tears; unparched, absorbing the agony of
this uninvited sense of loss
//
I have begged to leave Earth; this oxygen,
this ozone layer, this third planet from the sun
with hopes of finding a more tragic place
//
and I return home, shoes soaked in sludge
heavy with their drink, pulling me further into
the concave place
there is no such thing as a more tragic place.
I am here

Pray

Your type of love
makes my heart

s k i p

a beat
in the worst way
possible

Two words, two syllables.

The words, "I'm fine" have become

my favorite lie

the two words that hide the most

my oversized jacket hiding my secret

my smile fake, my heart cracked

my words silenced, my feet
burdened

but don't worry
I'm fine

Will?

Sometimes I beg
pray that you
will go away
and you never do
but
what happens
when the
universe finally
decides to listen
to me

Note to self

I need more from you

Something to notice

You look at me with zero expectations but yet

expect me to arrive in a particular manner;

head held high, shoulders back, standing tall

as if I have agreed to rise to the occasion
//
you expect me to accept the fact that you deceived

me into living in an exhibit

mistaken as the world

My request

You ask for a hug
my mind yells
screams
holds up warning signs
traffic signals; detour
"wrong way"
"stop"
but
I end up in your arms
anyway

.

Cinderella

Think lovely wonderful thoughts
they will lift you up

Disappointment

The weeds in the front lawn
that desire to someday be grass
roll its eyes at the sound
of the bottles clinking together

Deep within

I sit here at 12:31 p.m.
listening to your loud
obnoxious
voice
but
all
I
can
see
is
the
crashing
of waves
against
the
rocks

The thieves

Who told me what I deserved
who told me that I am only worthy
of the smallest amount of love
and
respect

who told me to accept the empty
apologies filled with fragmented
promises

who taught you to believe the
senseless compliments fed to you

who taught you these things
that would destroy your spirit

who told you that was what you
deserved

who told me

Little girl

Don't ever let
a man
make you feel
like he
is
the
only
one
who cares

One day

You will learn to
walk away from
things
people
hearts
that no longer
deserve any part
of you

Lies vs Love

I said
hold me
love me
accept me
cherish me
teach me
//
but instead you
tore
ripped
wrenched
burned
away everything I held on to

Something forced

My love for you
I don't want to
be
responsible for
holding your
happy
heart
when you
are responsible
for
drowning
mine

Possibilities

I'm afraid that getting

hurt by you isn't the

worst thing

but seeing you happy

laughing

playing

smiling

is because

that

should

be

me

Mute

The choir of bottles striking

singing

together paired with the slur

of your words

is the most

hideous song

played on your radio

Everyday

I shouldn't have
to make you
understand that I am
a person filled with life,
knowledge
and sometimes empty white space
//
empty white space that
should be my
holy place, common space
not based
or blinded
by your inebriated face

Bloom

It takes a special person to see that
nothing is quiet
the flames of love
(daughter father
mother daughter
daughter son
mother son
husband wife
husband husband
wife wife)
cannot be put out
with a simple bucket
of water

Daily mistakes

I try my hardest to hide the
hurt with a smile
because I don't want to
embarrass you

only if they knew...
you'd finally get hurt too

A tale of disregard

Perhaps the saddest
of all is that
these struggles have
outlived lives that
should still be breathing
//

Conscious torture

Her days oppression
cannot be eased by the solitude in night

Why?

Because that doesn't exist

Isolated Boulevard

I woke up heavy this morning
my mind was drowning
I tried talking, I choked on my
words and no one could hear me
screaming
my tears stained my heart and I
couldn't breathe
my whole body was throbbing and
pounding as I watched the time change
on the clock

my feet were discouraged and would not let
me move
my eyes were open but I was not seeing
my lungs were filling with air but I was
not living
my body was warm but I felt as dead as
a corpse

because of you

I did not live this day

Lavender

We begin as roots

      and have the potential
      to grow a stem
      color
      petals
            don't let him
            stunt your growth

Any minute now

I need to go to your
home
and fill every room
every space
with a new piece of furniture
make every plant and its' soil
damp with water
to satisfy your cup with coffee
wipe down the countertops
wash your sheets until they are
white
and
clean
again
let me
let me
and then I will close the blinds
shut the drapes
so no one
will know
what your
home
really
looks like

Sure.

You can be forgiven
I forgive you
she forgives you
we forgive you
but
you don't get a
second chance
to be who you
were supposed to be
from
the
start

On Sundays

So many flowers are begging to bloom where the sun doesn't shine

It's midnight

Stop this train

I remember

Everything
you
said
you
didn't
mean
//
do you

Guilty

Don't
ever
again
apologize
for his
actions

Purloin

I wanted you to fill
the spaces I could
not feel
that was a mistake

.

Recipe

tears
fears
years

Cracked concrete

I tried to run
away many times
but
every time my foot
hits the sidewalk
my lungs begin to
collapse
as if this air
is not good
and yours is better
I stay
because I
don't want you to
damage anyone else
this is why
I let you skin me
to the bone

Menace

When my phone vibrates
I get afraid
the thumping in my chest
gets louder and louder,
my ears begin to bleed as my
mind thinks of the possible
evils that hide on the other line
my breath gets caught in my
throat; it never makes it to
my
lungs and I wonder if the
unknown staying silent is
better than the screaming of
the known

I'm not sure
I always pick up

Not for you

You got mad at me
because I wasn't going
to be a weak woman
and stand at the base
of your tree
begging for the berries,
nuts, nectarines, a meal
like you wanted

I can feed myself you don't deserve my hunger

Home

He

left

I

breathed

Living dead

Perhaps you should
look at me
like you
//
know I
am still living

Cul-de-sac

Before I leave for work,
I make sure my house is
clean

just in case I don't make it
home tonight
//

.

Bed of roses

I wish I could spend
my time
worrying about something
that actually matters
instead
I worry and lose
sleep over
you

Waiting

I'm still waiting for sugar instead of salt

Tears

Yes
sometimes I cry
my eyes overflow with wet pain while my heart
overflows with release
I cry because it's all I can do when the world
seems too heavy to carry

//

but I'm not strong enough to stop my
breathing
wet pain
wet pain
wet pain
my wet pain
I hope it stains the wood

Us

You existed before the pain
and you will live long after
it

Narrative

You are *not* what I wanted
you are *not* what I asked for
you are *not* what I need

Birth/Origin

God gave me a big mouth

loud features

a strong stem
//
because he knew I would

have to yell and scream

bleed and fight

push and shove you

for my right to life

Power antonym

It's hard being a superhero
when you rip and shred my cape

Sunrise,, sundown.

The flowers can't bloom
won't bloom
if
//
they are being
suffocated
in a world
by air not
meant
for their
lungs

Unsteady

Your voice

I hear

will be

here and

I won't know

how to live

until it

disappears

Scars

Oh darling, don't you cry
let me water your stem.
When the world runs dry
remember you are a gem.

The war is over now,
let the sunshine in.

And breathe, breathe, breathe.

You've come so far
let the wind kiss your face
show me a piece of my heart
I'm hoping you will replace.

You don't have to fight now,
go close your eyes and rest

And breathe, breathe, breathe.

What you do.

Questions part II

Why did
you do
that what
did I do
are you
mad are
you okay
why can't
you be nice
what happened
to you
why did you
choose to
hurt me

Vacant calls

You wonder why
I don't talk
to you

why I let the
phone ring until
the world turns
silent

why my vocabulary
turns to single
digits when
you enter
the
space

I wonder why you
can't see the
damage you
have done

Soul

I don't know why I still want to cry
the well
has run dry
there is no water left
but my eyes still thirst for
rain

you make me feel like
sadness always needs to be
streaming down
my face

Title, no title.

Be careful where your garbage goes
it's important to remember when I
turn into an angel and attack
the sky

The unforgettable

I'm learning to
shut my mind
close the blinds
on the rooms
you occupy

I try
but you take
up so
much
space

Silence

One day you will look for her
light in the darkness
her warmth when your heart
is cold
and
you will be in pain because
she won't be
there
to keep you
warm

Funeral

You don't always need a knife to kill
you never had one and look
what you did to me

Selfish drowning

If she could show
you
how awful you
made her feel
if
the bruises on
her heart were
translated to
her skin
you
would never
be able to
look in her
eyes
again

Stonecold

The grass is
still greener
under the
calluses
on my
feet

Fairytale

You used to tell me
that I was a princess
your princess

but why
did you lock me
in the tower

R.I.P

This is a war I cannot win

Only nightmares

I used to dream about getting
married
being happy
raising a family
having dandelions grow in
my front yard
I don't dream anymore

Happily, Ever After

You've made me believe that I am not strong
enough good enough to save myself

now I am looking for a knight to save me

Shatterproof

You lied
and made
me think
you were
armored
indestructible

            but really
            behind the
            bottles you
            are the
            most broken
            of us all

Take it back

I asked for a kiss
you gave me poison

Dead

You make me afraid to sleep

and I am so tired

Life-life-(less)

I've written so much
about you
my pen is running
out of ink
i wonder
what
that
means
for

me

Carnation

I don't miss you as much
as I thought I would
because through it all
I have found that I
am all I need

A soldier's sentiment

Your lips are the
most powerful
yet destructive
force
//
I want to lick
the succulent words
dripping soundly from your
tongue
//
I want the coffee
you drink to burn
your taste buds
I want the cup you
drink from to cut
your tongue
so my name can't
find the entrance or
exit parting of your
lips
so that you can't call me
out of my name anymore

my name belongs to me

Don't

I feel the most
alone
lonely
sitting next to you

HIM

You decide
when I'm
good enough
to be seen

worth your time

You decide
when I'm
good enough
to talk to

worth your time

Introduction

I think she
is caught
between
who she is
and who she
wants
to be

Unspoken Sight

I can stare blankly
and it hurts
because I can see
it

I can still see
that it doesn't
affect you as
much as I think
it
should

and now my eyes
my eyes
have created a new
picture
of
who
you
are //

who you must be

Allie

When you start questioning your life
I dare you to
open your window and close your
mind

the branches are
dancing instead of breaking
the sun is living not burning
believe the leaves are rustling beautifully
because they choose to

they have a choice
so do you

that's what you have to do

Whiskey words II

I hear yelling through the walls.
I feel the words you spit rising
up through the floor where my feet locate for stability.
Your utterance loathed with foul adornment causes my
feet to ache and swell and burn from lumps and blisters.

I cry and cry
as I try running as far as I can from this burning
wood.
My feet singe and branded with your words of hate
have nowhere to go.
I want to warn others of people like you but I can't move.
The pain is unbearable.
But
I can't move.

You won't let me move.

Forget me not

I think about the times we used to laugh
but I don't miss them
because you were a stranger then

                              now I know who
                              you are

                              what you really
                              are

Control

This world
your world
your life
seemed
innocently
beautiful
//
but
I got too
comfortable
I got too
close
and it's
ghastly

You

Can find her broken on the bathroom floor

What it is

Every time you
take a sip
or
pour another
headache
you punch a
hole in my
heart
and watch
me
bleed

Owned

I try
to break
away, move
on, shut
the curtain
because I
know I
deserve better
but you
did a
great job-
everything
reminds
me of
you

Get Away

The air around you is so thick
I don't want to
contaminate my lungs
any longer

Unrequited Love

You can go days without
touching me
talking to me
seeing me
and I forgave you
yet
the one moment
the one time
I don't
touch you
talk to you
I'm a villain and
you look at me with so
much pain, eyes filled
with gloom, depression
as if someone was trying to
kill you
like I owe you something

Like
I
Owe
You

The Love I'm Given

Even
in my dreams
I spend time
picking
my teeth
one
by
one
out of the carpet

Repeat

I love you

I love you

        is your version of
        "I hate you
        watch out"

I was

You load the gun
aim
pull the trigger
and then act like
you
were the one who got
shot

Also you

Are responsible for putting
her on the bathroom floor
you twirl and sway with her
touching her hips
using the same two hands that
tortured broke and deposited
her on the cold bathroom floor

Via text

She unlocked/and held her breath
she opened/hate spit in her face
she read/the pain welled in her eyes
she cried/because she can't escape
and cried/you weren't even there
and cried/look what you did

I know it was because of
you

Oh, Father.

Son of God sun of the sky
I look up
weeping, begging, reaching
for the forgiveness fervent from
my Father
touch my soul tonight
66 books
from the sickly to the crucifix
relationships intermix
Omnipotent. Omnipresent.
Omniscient
hold my hand, guide my heart,
help
it all make
sense
//
when others mention your name
I become tense
present tense

~to those lost

Exist to die, die to live

She is bleeding from the inside and
combating the beast

~to those wrestling demons

Engulfed promises

Your vocabulary
is full of lies
I have
read
before

Failed Attempt

Your attempt
to be
kind
is being completely
overlooked
it's too late
I don't care how
hard
you try
the hate you spew
the evilness you have
shown
is all I see
so stop trying

Age 15

She never really had a clue how beautiful she was
the only thing she saw was the only thing she knew.
never was alone
//
her mind was made
she walks
the pain that clouded her day to day
she tried and she cried
she couldn't find the strength, she wish she could hide.
//
and fix all the things she couldn't see
she said
goodbye without a word

I wish she stayed

~to those searching

Dangerous power

I have fought a dragon before
I have climbed my way out of
the dungeon many times
I will find my way from you
just fine

Day after day.

You've done so much damage
I am a broken mirror
a heap of smashed glass
please
watch your step

yearning for someone to
stop using me
stop looking at me
stop questioning me

just throw me out

You'll be okay.

I hope one day
I will bloom

I hope one day
your whiskey fueled
words will roll silently
off my back

I hope one day
I will walk straight
again.

I hope
I hope

One day
you'll be okay

And I will too.

Made in the USA
Middletown, DE
02 September 2023